C000148744

The Year that Stole the Light Away

Brandon White

The Year that Stole the Light Away

Brandon White

Raw Earth Ink
2020

This book is a work of poetry.

Copyright 2020 by Brandon White

All rights reserved. No part of this book may be reproduced or used in any manner without express written permission from the author except in the case of quotations used in a book review in which a clear link to the source of the quote and its author is required.

First paperback edition May 2020

Cover design by Brandon White

ISBN 978-1-7330808-7-3 (paperback)

Published by Raw Earth Ink
PO Box 39332
Ninilchik, Alaska USA 99639
www.taracaribou.com

Prologue

I'll start by saying, this collection of poems was never supposed to exist.

My Father, Phillip White, was precisely the kind of man everyone hopes their father to be. He was hardworking, loving, selfless, and tough as nails. Dad was a High School State Champion in Football, an excellent baseball player, shuffleboard king, and master of fart humor. At 6'3" and 280lbs, he was a physically imposing figure, but always kind, unless given reason not to be. He was my best friend and the standard by which I measure myself as a man, husband, and Father.

Cancer took him in February of 2019.

Within these pages are my attempt at creating something of beauty and worth in a time of overwhelming sadness. If this work finds you in the throes of tragedy, I hope it serves as a reminder that, despite how lonely you might feel, you are anything but alone.

In Loving Memory of
Phillip Artie White
1954-2019

Foolishly we cling to hope

How could we not see

That we were tied to the tracks

All along?

A Storm Approaches

We spend so much time
wishing for success,
for luck, for the days
to pass easy;

we forget
to wish for
peaceful
endings.

Battle-hardened

I watch
as you make your way down the hall.
Short, careful steps;
like that of a child.

Your body
slumped to one side,
and your memory
isn't what it used to be.

The scars
on your head run deep
I follow them like a map
to simpler times.

Your voice,
though softened, still commands.
Your eyes, at times vacant,
still cut.

You have
the appearance
of a man familiar
with battle.

A soldier
returning home
in short, careful steps.
A victory march.

Panic

I suppose we're all due
at least one reminder
of the fragility
of life.

One that shakes us awake.
One that tunes the heartstrings,
strumming softly, so that we might
learn to love the song again.

One that darkens the sky,
and brings panic
at the first sign
of rain.

Dig

Every day I return,
shovel in hand,
and I dig.

I dig to keep my sanity.
I dig to find the sacred
words.

The words we etch
into flesh and
tombstones.

Words that will echo
across all the years
you'll never see.

Worry Whispers Softly

There's a worry in me
that can't be prayed away
or drugged into submission.

I feel it in my bones,
traveling up my arm and
across my back like electric shock.

I feel it slicing
through muscle, and tendon,
and confidence.

I hear it whisper to me
all through the night,
in a voice low and familiar;

like an old friend
who tells you terrible things
when they drink too much.

Thoughts from the Birthday Boy

As I place the final day
of my 31st year upon the fire,
I look around for anything
I might have left behind.

Confident that I'm ready,
I turn to face a future
void of form.

Like clay on a Potter's wheel,
the story takes shape
with every decision, big or small.

As if the path ahead
and the countless possibilities refused
had been laid long before

the first breath drawn into tiny lungs
was sent back into the world
in a primal, pitiful cry.

Tremble

This brownie tastes
like childhood.

Little Debbie sits in a warehouse
somewhere and wraps them individually.

Mom didn't buy them very often,
or any junk food for that matter.

You were younger then.
You were stronger then.

You're still the strongest man
I know.

Even as your legs tremble
beneath you.

My Father the Mountain

I suffer from regular heartbreak.
Never more so than when helping you
perform simple tasks.

I support your hulking frame as you walk,
a trail of urine behind us,
you don't seem to notice.

You're unsteady.
Your body weakened
beyond recovery.

I'm reminded
of a great mountain
disfigured by erosion.

You still cast a tremendous shadow,
and I'm still the little boy
staring up in awe.

The Coffee Sat Cold

Burrow
deep into my skull
and dig out this anxiety.
I've lost hours
now.

Scoop out a bad memory
or two while you're at it.
I have a habit
of reliving my regrets
when I should be resting.

When I woke today for the second time,
my coffee sat cold where I'd left it.
Before sleep pulled
me back into its depths.
Where all the healing is.

The Great Unsinkable

My love,
we have become
like a boat upon troubled water;

crashed upon
and tossed about
by forces indifferent.

Huddled together,
shaking in each other's arms,
waiting for the next wave.

And yet we float on.
The great unsinkable
two.

Diagnosis

We live quiet, simple lives,
blissfully unaware
of the chaos lurking
just beneath the surface.

Our flesh plays the role
of a gracious host
until we've overstayed
our welcome,

and the vessel
betrays the master.

Guarantees

If pain is our only guarantee
and suffering a necessity,
then surely love,
in all its complexity,
is the face of God
revealed.

Hands

I don't know
if I've ever noticed
how similar our hands are.

The fingers,
the knuckles,
the way they tremble.

Oblivious

People talk loudly
in hospital hallways.

They're oblivious to the suffering
that surrounds them;

to the people having conversations
they never thought they'd have,

making decisions they never thought
they'd have to make.

Betrayal

I don't want to be angry.

I don't want to be bitter.

I don't want to shake
my fist at God.

I want to be strong enough
to bear the burden.

I'm following
your wishes,

so why does this feel
like a betrayal?

Blue Walls

There are chips in these
blue walls.

The same shade as your daughter's room
so many years ago.

The nurses seem
nice enough.

Across the hall, a man snores loudly
and thrashes in his blankets.

A picture of the Ozarks
waits to greet you when you wake,

and next to your bed,
a tan pleather chair

where I sit,
watching your chest rise and fall

learning the value
of every moment.

The Best Kind of Friend

I'm sitting at a bar
with the best kind of friend.

The kind that doesn't ask
too many questions.

The whiskey burns.

The beer soothes.

I didn't come here to escape.

I know better.

You're everywhere I go.

One More

This Super Bowl was the worst
I've seen.

I hate that you missed it, but you deserved
a better game.

I had hoped to to share one more
with you.

One more game, one more drink,
one more night that stretched on too long,

but the morphine has
carried you off

to simpler times,
a simpler life.

The Big Clock

The big clock is burning,
and slowly collapsing in on itself.

All we can do is watch as the only life
we've known comes to an end.

Your name now rests
on the lips of eternity.

A gentle voice will soon
cut through the suffering

and call a good man
home.

Cold

The air outside is still and cold.

The kind of cold that eats through your clothes,
through your shoes.

The kind of cold that seems strangely alive
and malicious.

If it's come for my heart,
it will find only the fire of a man

who refuses to bow
to his uncertainty.

Strength

They don't make a pill for this.

They don't have a pamphlet
that makes sense of it.

Whiskey is a loyal companion,
but it doesn't stop the dreams.

Do you still dream?

Curled up like a child
beneath your blanket.

You still open your eyes
when I tell you I love you.

You still find the strength
to say it back.

Drown

Do you know how many memories
you can fit into a single closet?

Thousands.

Maybe millions.

An entire lifetime's worth,
or two if you were interesting enough.

All this and you'd still have room
for someone to sit comfortably

and drown.

A Simple Man

I am a simple man
who's in love with his simple life,

with the laughter of his children.

with the heart of a good woman.

I am a simple man
who's slowly coming undone.

Crushed against the weight
of inevitability,

and unable to write about
true grief,

the worst days of my life,

without feeling a bit
melodramatic.

Salvation

No one comes to salvation
without suffering.

How could one know
true gratitude
without first knowing
what it is to sit in this chair,
waiting for your eyes to open?

Will you know me when they do?
If they do?

No.

No one comes to salvation
without suffering.

Don't Worry

I cradle you
as you cradled me

32 years and
2 months ago.

Doing the dirty work one does
for someone they love

with a heart full of pity
and a mind that will never shake the image.

I whisper in your ear,
over and over,

I've got you.

Don't worry.

Rest Easy

Every time you open your eyes
someone new is sitting beside you.

Idiots and angels,
the indifferent and I.

Rest easy,
you have nothing to fear.

I'll bury anyone foolish enough
to do wrong by you.

Terrified

We lift the sheet
on the count of three
and move you
onto your side.

You stare
at the ceiling, silent.
I attempt a joke,
it falls flat.

I'm terrified of what's
happening behind your eyes.

I don't want
to know.

Hum

The hospital bed hum
is somehow soothing.

I catch myself wanting
to fall asleep if I stay too long.

You rest most of the time
so I suppose I'm not hurting anything.

Some days I choose
to stand and watch

as you lay
like a broken Christ.

Your holy words written
on my heart.

The words of a man
who took up his cross.

Anchor

Please don't take your hand away.

Keep it right here.

Anchor me to reality.

The feeling of your fingers,

the vibration of the car,

the soft breathing of sleeping children.

A mind in overdrive.

A churning stomach.

A man burning.

Lying Awake

At night before bed
I take the weight from my shoulders
and hold it to my chest.

As it presses down
my breathing becomes
laborious.

Thoughts
become jumbled
but I can't let go.

I just hold tighter
and wait for sleep
to find me.

Cocktail

Morphine and Ativan.

Both can be absorbed beneath the tongue.

A powerful cocktail.

I hold you to me while they change the pillows.

Tears fall from my cheeks and land on your sleeve.

I hope you don't notice.

I won't let you see.

I lay my head to your chest and listen to you breathe

while the world around me burns.

Balance

My whiskey glass balances on my chest
as I type this to you now.

I'm wondering what lesson hides
in how our minds and bodies fall apart.

In how we make sense of a loss
we can't even speak of

without
shaking hands.

Minutes

My days melt into one another.

I have no real sense of time, the day,
or how long we've been doing this.

All I'm counting are the minutes
you lay awake.

The moments where I can take your hand
and feel a squeeze of acknowledgment

and feel as they're
ripped away.

Shell-Shocked

This bedroom has become
a battlefield.

Where the presence of life and death
weigh heavily in equal measure.

Where momentum changes and shifts
in our favor and out within seconds.

Where a great war has consumed
our years

and left us shell-shocked
and sweating in our sleep.

Jumping at the sound of every cough
like it was gunfire.

A Hummingbird's Wings

Do you hear that?

What is it?

The beating of your heart?

It sounds to me,

like a hummingbird's wings
come to carry you off.

Follow the sound.
You've fought well.

There's no fiery torment there.
No judgement.

Only peace
and reconciliation.

Your mother's arms,
open and waiting.

More

You have become more.

More than flesh,
or fingers,
or warm hands.

More than morphine,
or pills,
or radiated bones.

You have become more.

More than grief,
or raw nerves,
or unbearable loss.

You have become more.

Reflection

32 years ago,
you welcomed me into this world.

32 years later,
I held your hand and led you out of it.

Your life
and death

were beautiful
poetry.

The Messenger

Yesterday,
a woman came to my mother's door
and said,

I died once.
I wanted you to know
he's okay now.

Perhaps someday,
when this life becomes recognizable,
we'll be okay too.

The Face Behind My Eyes

The door keeps swinging open.
Frigid air blows in,
putting my bones on ice.

My arms ache.
My fingers are stiff with cold.
I've stood long in the presence of death,

and now I see your face
every time
I close my eyes.

Inch

You were one of billions
of people making their way
through the world.

Loving, caring, drinking
and dreaming.

The world
doesn't stop when
a soul departs.

But I did.

I haven't moved an inch.

The Box

Light cuts
through the blinds in the room
where I did my best
for you.

I stand before a small wooden box.
Beautiful crosses carved into each side.
I speak to it
in hushed tones.

My finger
traces each cross.
This is all
I have of you now.

Dreams of Home

Last night I dreamt
of overcast skies and a runny nose

that I wiped with my sleeve
before pulling my arms into my shirt.

I forgot my coat again,
the cold air stings my eyes

as I pedal faster.
The streetlights buzz to life,

as the sun settles behind the
trees at the end of Kingsley Place.

I'm trying to make it home
before dark.

Your voice calls for me.
I pedal faster.

I see you standing in the driveway,
I pedal faster.

I want to see your face, to hear your voice,
I pedal faster.

I wake before I reach you.
Grief has become my world.

Restored

I expect you

to come through the door

any minute now.

For heavy footsteps

to echo

through the house.

For you to

appear

restored.

Grief is a Strange Bird

I

Grief
is a strange bird
circling overhead,
swooping down,
flying out of sight
and back again.

II

Did you know that 12 weeks
is a significant mark
when dealing with loss?
They say that's when reality begins to set in,
as if life could be reassembled
in a few simple steps.

The truth is that grief is a strange bird
perched on an overflowing box of t-shirts
in a hot garage.
Sloppily taped and easily torn open.
Press your face into the cloth
and see what remains.

III

I'm eating this sandwich slowly.
White bread, turkey, cheese, and chips.
A classic American lunch
known to thousands of working folk
who aren't sure what became of the life
they thought they'd live,
but I'm not thinking of that now.

I'm considering bringing
your ashes to the table
and placing them across from me.
You see, grief is a strange bird
you catch out of the corner of your eye
that takes whatever progress you've made
back to zero.

IV

It's a sucker-punch from
an invisible opponent.
It's using every ounce of will
to hold yourself together,
because breaking down
in front of strangers
is not an option.

It's needing to write the poem
because will-power might not be enough.
You see, grief is a strange bird
trailed by dark clouds
that blot out the sun
and bring your world
to a halt.

A kiss upon a cooling forehead

Letting go of fingers

already purple

The war is over.

Kaleidoscope Pain

Billions of atoms converge
to create an out-of-shape
32-year-old down on his back.

A true miracle of nature.

I close my eyes
when the pain comes.

Kaleidoscope visions
flash behind my eyelids.

I've always wanted
colors I could feel.

Remember

I remember block parties
and bicycle spokes.

I remember the sting
of pool water in my nose.

I remember the first girl
that made me nervous.

I remember Christmas morning
and waking you up before sunrise.

I remember countless trips
to Grandma's house, just us two.

I remember Springsteen concerts,
and football games.

I remember beer
and shuffleboard.

I remember how you
always believed in me.

It hurts to
remember.

Smile

The leaves tremble
like beaten dogs
as the wind carries in
our third storm in two days.

I sit in my car counting the minutes
until I return to work while
Opus 15 by Dustin O'Halloran
plays softly.

I stare into the unblinking eyes
of the girl from the store advertisement banner.
Smiling her eternal smile.
Smiling like nobody smiles.

Nobody.

A Pocket Full of Ireland

I keep Ireland in my pocket
in case of emergencies.

The Cliffs of Moher
and the Dark Hedges.

A pint of Guinness,
a cigarette, and a song.

The air thick
with poetry.

Whistling drunk down
Grafton Street.

All the possibilities of life
lay open before me

and death is but a distant,
hazy dream.

The Inevitable Reclamation

I am here to bear witness
to the undoing
and fall of great men.

I am here to bear witness
to the crumbling of idols
and the death of childhood dreams.

I am here to bear witness
to the final breath of true art
and the fading of the song.

I am here to bear witness
to the inevitable
reclamation of truth.

Up in Smoke

I rewatch the movies
we enjoyed together
in hopes of sparking
some memory long forgotten.

I watch them and imagine
you seeing them for the first time,
with so many years
ahead of you.

I'm watching Up in Smoke now.
Up in Smoke like our time together.
Up in Smoke like these
earthly bodies.

I wish I could have known you
as a younger man.

Movie Sunday

I leave the chaos of home
for the chaos of the big screen,
where a 400-foot radioactive lizard
wipes cities off the map.

Boston looks like my living room
by the end of the film,
and soon I'm back in my car
taking in a moment of silence.

On the drive home I'm met
with dozens of existential questions
that I try and offset with music
that seems to have lost it's magic.

I pull into the driveway and let
the car idle a while,
trying to clear my head
before heading inside

where all my love
waits patiently.

Small Changes

We used to drive this road,
half asleep and unaware
that our time was
slipping away.
The familiar landscape
forever changed by an
eruption of modern suburbia.

You can still see the stadium
from the road.
I can't remember the last time
I went to a game.
We used to go almost every
Friday night.
The team was renamed recently.

Small changes act
as a reminder that the world
has a way of moving on.
But what does that matter
to one now reconciled
with the creator
and all that must be?

The Year that Stole the Light Away

Your chair is where you left it.
No one sits there anymore.
It feels
disrespectful.

There's a painting of a horse
in the hallway now,
everything else is as it was.
Frozen in February.

I thought I'd ask if I could take the chair
as there was talk of getting rid of it.
I don't know if I could stand it.
It could never feel like mine.

I miss you so goddamn much.
I spend my nights drinking wine
until I can't keep my eyes open,
then fall into a deep sleep,

where I dream of
a great mountain.

The train has passed

And I'm dragging myself by my teeth

To gather the pieces of me scattered about

What a fucking mess.

Wild Young Heart

There was a strong wind today,
it blew the trees to awkward angles.

It took the cold from the air
and the clouds from the sky.

I stood holding you,
watching your hair blow back.

You held out your arms
as if inviting another gust.

With little eyes full of wonder,
a wild young heart embraces the world.

Seesaw

Seesaw

The balance of your mind.

Seesaw

See something profound and know
that what you saw has changed you
forever.

Seesaw

See the saw and know that there's
nothing holding you down
that can't be cut away.

Broken Blinds

You watch the world through
broken blinds with a desire
to understand

the nature of the wind blowing through the trees.
Trees that reach towards the sky
like hands in worship.

To know the reason
for each drop of rain
tapping against the window.

Your young mind
drawing conclusions
far more beautiful than reality.

You don't filter the world
through a broken heart
and I envy you for it.

Leaks

There's a hole in the ceiling
where a leak became
something more.
It's a black eye for a beautiful room.

We sip tea while waiting
for our sandwiches.
My eyes drift back
to the ceiling.

You've never been here.
I hyped it up too,
not realizing it was partially
caved-in.

We discuss the future,
and dance around a sadness
we still can't wrap
our minds around.

All because a small spot
on a CT scan became something more.

Promises

Remember this moment
when the old life
calls to you again.

Remember your brokenness,
and the promises
you made in the dark.

Remember the final breath
and the frantic heartbeat
under your hand.

Remember how quickly
a life, with all it's complexity,
can vanish.

I Want to be Remembered

I just want to be remembered
as a good man,
and to die
bravely.

What else
is there to hope for?
What else
could possibly matter?

My father
was an excellent example
in living,
and in dying.

Becoming

I do my best with the hour a day
I'm afforded to do my work.
I'm better for my limitations.
I listen closer.
I take the time to observe
without feeling the need to qualify
whatever plays out
before me.

For this brief time,
I melt into, and am at one
with darkness and light alike.
All of the wonderful pain,
the devastating love,
It all has its place.
We are endlessly
becoming.

A Bag Full of Wendy's,
A Head Full of Rage

A poorly timed stream of oncoming headlights
sparks new rage.
Gritting teeth,
a white-knuckled grip,
each driver equally worthy
of my wrath.

My hands still smell of
hospital sanitizer
and I can't shake this cold.
There's no rest for parents
who carry the weight of worry
for an ill child.

Goddamn this year.
Tornados, and cancer,
and thirty-plus doctor's visits,
unspeakable grief,
and sleepless nights.
GODDAMN THIS YEAR!

My fist connects with
the center of the steering wheel,
sending a sharp blast from
the car horn into an endless night
and possibly causing the man
in the Dodge across from me to shit himself.

Tears flow.
I should be
out of tears by now.
I should be
out of hope by now.
But here I am.

I'll hate this poem
in the morning.

Nature

My feet touch forbidden blacktop
about 30 feet from the crosswalk
they prefer you use.
Behold my only
act of rebellion today.
My small way of setting fire
to the world.
Really, I'm just impatient.

The roasted duck soup
left a strange taste in my mouth,
like cruel words.
The cold air feels electric
and helps to push me forward.
Up and down the avenue I go,
resisting the pull of each passing bar
and warm thoughts of good rye.

Hear me now;
I long for nothing.
Not for love or understanding.
Not for pity or prayer.
I have accepted my nature.
Born to wander.
Born to wonder.
Born to sit in the burning room

unblinking.

God's House & the Lone Coyote

The steam from my coffee
fogs up the small panes of glass
in the backdoor.
I often stand here in the morning,
staring out at the frozen world.

Chain link separates our backyard
and an empty field.
Beyond the field a firehouse,
and a church.
I wish it were just the field.

I guess I'm thankful
that help
is no more than
a hundred yards
away at any moment,

and having
God's house
in the neighborhood
should do wonders for
my property value.

I watch a lone
coyote make his way
across the frozen grass
just beyond
the back fence.

He pauses and
looks back the way he came,
as if reconsidering the choice
that brought him here.

Eventually, he carries on.
I sip my coffee.
The morning sun ascends.
The world turns.

Purify

I'm burning in this skin.
I am molten steel,
fire and brimstone,
and every other
cliché one might
pick from the lowest
of low hanging branches
to try and convey
their anger.

Fuck you, Forrest Gander
and your Pulitzer Prize too.
Fuck your extended vocabulary
and your brilliant mind.
Did you even consider
that you might make
someone insecure with
work like that?
I bet not!

Sigh...
I'm sorry, Mr. Gander.
The truth is, I respect you
a great deal, but this
anger needs somewhere to go.
This fist needs drywall.
These teeth need a throat.
This tongue needs the name
of the one(s) responsible.

Bury the old life!
Bring down the idols
with cancer-causing
weed killer.
Line the pockets
of evil men
and bring a tear
to the eyes of God.

If revenge is a fool's game,
I'll gladly play the part.
I'll tear through every
Tom, Dick, and Harry
floating through a shit life,
getting half-hearted hand-jobs
from wives they haven't
loved in years;
I'll ease their suffering.

Forrest Gander, I am not.
Just one among the brokenhearted
unable to come to terms;
a clown who longs to burn kings.
This rage, my God, the rage;
I'm a fly in the web
and a spider inches
closer.

Guilt

I was scrolling through the news
the other day when I came across an article
entitled, *Thinking Too Much Might Kill You.*
If that's the case,
there's no question,
I'm toast.

Tomorrow's your birthday
and the first of many traditions
to be marked since your passing.
I hadn't noticed the date.
I had to be reminded.
I feel guilty about that.

I don't know that I'm ready
to reopen the wound,
but then again,
I wasn't ready
for much of what's happened
this year.

I was able to think of you yesterday
without sadness.
Without the unbearable weight of loss.
I was able to smile,
and remember,
and be grateful.

But tonight
the tears
and the guilt
have found me again.
I don't want to feel
like I'm leaving
you behind.

Whispers

I opened my eyes this morning
without the familiar throb behind them.
I didn't take Advil, or Pepto Bismol,
or follow any part of the carefully crafted
regimen that insures I'm able to
fulfill my responsibilities.

I opened my eyes this morning
without the hollow feeling in my chest.
I didn't shed a tear in the shower,
or while brushing my teeth, or
at any point during my ritual of
preparing for work.

I opened my eyes this morning
understanding that you're gone,
and yet closer than you've ever been.
Knowing that if I listen close enough,
you're still here; guiding me
in holy whispers.

The Musings of a Future Yelper

They've never been able to
maintain a restaurant at this location,
and many have tried.

It's not a bad spot, either.
Downtown, right on the avenue,
the best bars within walking distance.

I've sampled every establishment
that attempts to put roots down here.
They've all been decent enough.

For whatever reason,
the people won't come.
Sushi, Burgers, Piano Bar, it makes no difference.

I've sampled cuisine
from four different countries
and sat in the same shitty booth each time.

Outside, the rain falls steadily.
It'll be this way for the next several days, and I'm sad
my daughter might not get her last train ride of the season.

Three men enter the restaurant
and sit directly
in my line of sight.

Above me, a TV plays sports highlights
and when they watch, it feels like
they're staring.

Maybe they are?
I've reached that elusive point in life
where it makes no difference.

The burger and fries
are too salty.
What a shame.

My waitress asks how everything tastes,
and I lie to make her feel better.
She smiles her crooked smile and fixes her peroxide-blonde hair.

I ask for my ticket
and she's out of sight again.
I begin to review my latest poem.

I'm writing about food a lot lately.
I'll be yelping before
you know it.

Outside the rain pours on,
gathering into puddles,
and flowing down the drain.

Like all the wasted minutes
in a life.

Forgotten Gods & Checkerboard Smiles

I step into a crisp autumn afternoon
and, for a brief moment,
fall in love with the whole
damn world.

The downtown sidewalk is empty.
No tweaked-out, greasy-haired
backpackers recreating the dance from *Thriller* - that was yesterday.

Today it's just me,
my thoughts,
and the cars whizzing down
the avenue.

I step into a nearby Thai joint,
where beef fried rice and a glass of Sprite
is placed in front of me
within twelve minutes.

I watch the steam rise from the plate,
following it until I lock eyes with a giant Native American face
painted onto the building
across the street.

Great Cherokee eyes watch unblinking,
some forgotten god
stripped of authority and regulated
to street decoration.

They're into history in this town.
A few blocks from here,
a reconstruction of Judge Parker's gallows
draws a daily crowd.

86 people met their maker
at the hands of the Hanging Judge.
We gather there now to
see if any excitement still lingers in the air.

I finish my rice, pay the waiter, and leave.
As I walk out the door
two street folk on bicycles
nearly plow into me.

They laugh, and one looks back grinning,
every other tooth missing from his mouth.
His smile reminds me
of a checkerboard.

I tilt back my head
and take a deep breath of cold air.
Peace is always playing
hard to get.

I smile to myself,
proud of how I'm not letting the drugged-up bikers from hell ruin
my good mood.

There's only the smallest part of me
that hopes they pop a tire
and eat shit on
the sidewalk.

Some would call that progress.

Mini-Train Moping

I'm sick to my stomach
as the mini-train
begins its second trip
around the park.
It's not the ride so much
as it's me kicking my own ass
for using a word
too often in a poem.

How silly is that?
Such a simple mistake
and I rake myself over coals
and razor wire.
I don't want to be
a good writer.
I want to be
a great writer.

That old cliché is why
I treat myself
like this.
It's not a good excuse.
I've set traps throughout
my life that allow
for regular bouts
of self-loathing.

My daughter presses
her head into my chest.
She's sat quietly in my lap
the whole time.
Her sister is much more
excited about the ride.
She raises little hands
to the sky and squeals.

I often feel I can do no wrong
in their eyes,
just as my father
could do no wrong in mine.
I rest my chin on
the part between little pigtails
and take a deep breath,
a feeling of gratitude washing over me.

This is the only victory
to be had,
and the only one
of consequence.
To love and be loved
without condition
or qualification;
to be worthy of that love.

A Turkey Sandwich
and a Herd of Wild Children

I love the rain,
but if the person in front of me
doesn't speed up,
this may be the day I snap.

I've places to go,
people to see.
That's what Dad used
to say.
He was a patient man
for the most part.
I'm more like the calm moment
before an explosion.

My eyes are incredibly heavy.
Sleep's been hard to come by.
I'm anxious and bored with
writing about it.

I am thankful for
the change in weather.
The heat and humidity
had overstayed their welcome.

The leaves will change soon.
I used to think of falling leaves
as a kind of
slow death.

It's nothing more than
trees protecting themselves.
Shedding the unnecessary
to survive.

I'm sitting in my car
as I write to you now.
I've got a belly full of
turkey sandwich,

and I just looked up
to see a herd of school children
marching towards my car.
They stopped five feet from me.

Their teacher is explaining
street art to them and is
extremely animated.
A cameraman is filming it all.

The kids don't give a shit.
They're just happy
to be out
of class.
One of them is staring
because I saw him pick his nose.
I stare back with a look that says,
I know your secret.

It's starting to rain again,
so they're gathering the herd
and ushering them to
a nearby building.

Did I mention I love the rain?
How it washes away the unwanted?
How the electricity clings to the air
after a storm?

How it feels like another chance?

The Oldest Busboy in Town

I watch him bussing the tables
of this greasy cafe.
He's 69 years old,

his wife died years ago.
He's paid under the table
and lives in the owner's garage.

He pays the owner's cable bill
with his
pitiful wages.

He's not allowed to use
the house shower,
so he's given a wash bucket

which, according to his
description, is every bit
as shitty as it sounds.

He's clueless
to government assistance
and also buys the owner's groceries.

He drives an old van
from 40 miles outside of town
to the restaurant.

Sometimes he gives
the owner a lift
and pays for the gas.

I tell him he's being manipulated,
and living a sort of
slave existence.

He smiles, laughs,
shakes his head and says,
Oh, it's not so bad.

I can't help him.
He doesn't want my help.
He's just burning down the days.

It's crazy the things
people will tell you
because you smiled at them.

I'm too damn nice.

Blood Drive Blues

I winced as the needle
entered my arm.
Are you okay?
I'm fine, thanks.

He meant well in asking, but I
was still embarrassed he'd noticed.
I leaned back and tried to relax,
sipping a can of Gatorade.

How've you been?
I've been all right, you?
I knew what he meant.
We'd both lost our fathers this year.

We've known each other for a while,
but we don't often speak.
We shared stories
about how we were coping.

My eyes kept drifting
back to the small bag
that hung
near my arm.

My Dad used to give blood
fairly often.
I hadn't thought about
that before now.

I've heard that frozen
blood can be kept for ten years.
Does that mean
some part of you is still here?

A few pints of you
in some dark freezer?
That some stranger's
walking around with you in their veins?

That you're still pumping
through a strong heart, somewhere?
I didn't share these thoughts
with my friend.

All done!
The needle slid out of my arm.
I hold a bandage
where the needle had been,

hand raised to the sky
as if in worship.
I step out of the
donation bus and into the rain.

I should've had them
take more.
Maybe they would've
taken these thoughts with it.

Monday Morning Ritual

Monday mornings come
easier these days.
No headaches,
or burning eyes.

Hot water pours over me
and fills the bathroom with steam.
I wipe it away from the mirror
and take a look at myself.

There's a transformation
that must occur.
I shave the weekend stubble,
and slick back my hair.

I usually lose fifteen minutes here.
There's a lot to sort through
before the ritual
is complete.

I stare at my hands,
one is gripping a toothbrush.
I think of my father's hands,
mine still seem small in comparison.

His hands were
frail in the end,
though he still had one hell of a grip.
Those hands are gone now.

I take a deep breath.
This house is too damn quiet.
I need the laughter of my children.
I need the chaos, the distraction.

There's an
anger in me.
I feel it in waves,
burning and directionless.

My heart
holds a grudge
against an intangible
foe.

I wipe the tears
from my eyes,
dress,
and head out.

I'm looking for a way
to love
the world
again.

Bad Burgers and Barkers

$37.00 for cheeseburgers
and air rich with the smell
of cow shit can only mean
one thing;

The fair's in town.

They come from all walks of life
to deep fry everything in sight,
drink cheap beer,
and be taken by the barkers.

Step right up!
Win a prize!
Play the game!
See the show!

There's no way in hell
that whatever's in that tent
is better than what's
out here.

Ticket for a dollar!
Thirty for Twenty-six!
Talk about a deal!
A prize for the little lady?!
I try to make it out every year.
Not for the rides,
or the food,
just to be here.

The fair is one place
where a Saturday night
feels like it did
when I was younger;

Ripped open and full
of possibility.
Electric and
dangerous.

A barker calls out to me,
his hand full of darts;
Pop the balloon, win a prize!
Pop three, pick from the top shelf!

What do I win if
I put it between your eyes?
I ask in passing.
He stops barking.

Sunday Morning Musings

The sun rising over Rena Road helps me to forget
how much I don't like living here.
The street is usually empty this early
on Sunday mornings.
The houses, calm from the outside,
are full of families dressing for
service at one of the
81 churches in town.

As for me, I make my way
down the road slowly;
enjoying the way the cold air
sticks to my skin.
My head, throbbing from
last night's wine,
stuffed with thoughts
of everything
I wish I could change,

of everything I still might.

Corridor

It's not often you dream for other people.
Its not often other's dream on my behalf.
You can find some version of me here,
just beyond the maze of your mind, or mine.

There's time.
There's not enough time.
There's no time.
Time doesn't apply here.
That's it.

You've tapped into something.
You navigate long corridors,
to find some version of me waiting;
to share a moment of fellowship

and raise a glass
to all that waits
beyond the flesh.
It can be this simple.
I swear.

Bad Dreams and the Broken Rabbit

A flash of white was all I saw
before my back tire jumped
slightly.
I looked in my rearview with
a sense of dread in my gut,
and saw the small rabbit
dragging itself back
the way it'd came.

I immediately felt horrible.
For as long as I can remember,
I've had an unusual sensitivity
towards animals.
It doesn't keep me from eating them,
I just feel bad doing it.
A bit hypocritical,
I know.

Still, seeing this poor creature
dragging its busted body
made me sick with shame.
I saw something of myself
in the broken rabbit
and I quickly tried to push
the image from
my mind.

Later that night
while lying in bed,
I replayed the incident
again and again.
First I saw the rabbit,
then slowly,
I became
the rabbit.

I was watching the taillights
of the car that hit me
drive away, indifferent
to my pitiful state.
I laid on my back,
blood in my mouth,
and knew in my heart
I was alone.

There will be no rescue.
Survival, after all,
is a solitary
endeavor.

Holiday Blues #3

I torpedoed the night before Christmas
with enough Xanax to knock those
Sugar Plum Fairies
on their asses.
It wasn't intentional.
Doctor's orders.
Doctors, as you probably know,
are often full of shit.

Christmas went by in flashes
of red and green.
There were hugs and headaches
and laughing children.
There was wine and food,
and an unspoken sadness
that filled the space
you would've occupied.

I don't want to write about missing you.
I want to write about my hatred
for the abuse of adverbs,
or something witty about reindeer.

But I do miss you.
Terribly.
It'll be a year
in February.

I don't want to write about
how fucking low I felt today
after seesawing my brain
with little pink pills.

But that's where I'm at;
My children crawling over me,
laughing and smiling,
I use every ounce of will to rise to the occasion.

I'll be 33 on the 28th.
Where do I want to eat?
Do I want to eat?
Do I want to acknowledge it at all?

A big part of me wants to sit here
with a bottle of Old Forester
and drink until
I'm breathing smoke.

Silent night, holy night,
all is calm after a stiff rye.
I hope to see you when I finally sleep,
in dreams of heavenly peace.

No Alternative

This food is awful.
I knew it would be.
Time constraints
are dictating my dining today.

I'm emerging from the depths
of a considerable depression
brought on by the holidays,
perhaps even loosening the grip of grief.

The last couple of days have felt
like the slow burning off of dense fog.
The world taking shape around me,
all at once familiar and alien.

I've refused to accept my life
for what it's become,
and what I've learned
is that there's no alternative.

I can embrace an unfamiliar world,
a new year, the first to go unseen
by my father,
or self-destruct in magnificent fashion.

I want to be grateful again.
I want to be forgiven.
I want to feel the electricity of inspiration
sparking within me.

I want to know again,
the feeling of possibility.
The possibility of contentment.
The possibility of a little less pain.

Shock this tired heart back to beating.
There's still a life
here to be
lived.

Sewn together with carpet thread

I carry you on in every heartbeat

With every breath

I carry you on.

Acknowledgments

Thanks to my wife and partner in crime, Kenzie, whose continued encouragement of my creative endeavors and dedication to our family is so greatly appreciated. Through my darkest hours, your love has been the one constant on which I could rely.

To my lovely daughters, my little birds, Quinn and Scarlet, you are loved beyond description. You were two years old at the time this book was published. Should you eventually discover it as you navigate your lives, I hope it serves as a reminder to always be brave. The only person who can keep you from your dreams is the one staring back at you in the mirror.

To my mother, Jacqueline, who is strength beyond strength and love beyond love. Thank you for all you do and all you've done.

To my dear friend, Holly W (Instagram: _ontheline_), for your time and patient ear. I adore your writing and count myself lucky to know the blessing of your friendship.

To tara caribou for your encouragement and belief in this collection to which I am forever grateful.

To the many wonderful friends, writers, musicians, oracles, and sages that grace and shape my life. You fill my heart.

Brandon White

Made in the USA
Coppell, TX
16 January 2021

48232655R00067